John D. Cadore

THE HABITS OF CONSISTENCY
PERSEVERANCE
AND APPRECIATION

Other Books by this Author

Seven Years of Tribulation

The Road to Recovery

John D. Cadore books may be ordered through booksellers or by contacting

Law Office of John D. Cadore
34 Chenango Street
Binghamton, NY 13901
Ph. 607 777 9407
Cell 607 725 2150

ISBN: 979-8-9882493-0-6 (Paperback)
ISBN: 979-8-9882493-1-3 (eBook)

Table of Contents

DEDICATION

This book is dedicated to my oldest sister, Catherine Cadore. I wrote it after attending her funeral on August 23, 2022, on the island of Grenada, West Indies.

The three words in the title, Consistency, Perseverance and Appreciation are good descriptions of her life. Catherine went to be with the Lord on July 7, 2022, at the age of 77.

I have known Catherine all of my life and I have never heard her say anything bad about anyone. It is very hard and almost impossible to say that someone had no favorites, but to the best of my knowledge, she had no favorite person. She loved all her family equally, and all her friends in the same manner.

Catherine has inspired me to write this book.

THE HABITS OF CONSISTENCY
PERSEVERANCE
AND APPRECIATION

CHAPTER 1

CONSISTENCY

The Merriam-Webster dictionary defines consistency as "marked by regularity, or steady continuity" and "showing steady conformity to character, profession, belief, or custom."

In layman's language the word consistency means never giving up, or not abandoning one's course of action. For any consistent behavior or cause of action to be beneficial to the participant, or to anyone who adheres to the principle of being consistent, the activity, or activities being undertaken must be lawful, productive, and worthwhile. It is unproductive to oneself and to society if the activities being engaged in are illegal or fail to increase the economic welfare of the participant, or of society.

The general rule is that any activity that increases the economic well-being of the participant, or an individual, will also serve to increase the economic well-being of society at large.

Persistency means always performing one's assignments and obligations. This includes occasions when one is not in the mood for doing so, or simply does not feel like partaking in the assignments or obligations. In the long run, individuals should be able to rely on you to perform your assignments and obligations. You would eventually be viewed by many as someone that is credible and reliable.

Credibility and reliability are both necessary traits for success in almost every endeavor and walk of life.

For this reason, one can readily conclude that participation in illegal or unproductive activities is detrimental to the participant, and to society at large. One can also conclude that participation in any form of illegal drug trade is unproductive and detrimental to society at large. Participation in any form of illegal drug operation, although it may yield financial rewards to the participants, carries with it the real and constant threat of incarceration. Additionally, any form of illegal drug trade will usually serve to bring destruction to families and decay to society.

For the above-mentioned reasons, individuals should commit to being consistent in self-fulfilling and society-building activities. Being consistent would generally mean sticking to the plan and performing the activities even when one is not in the mood to do it or does not feel like doing it.

THE CONSISTENCY OF TITHING AND SAVING

Within the Christian community it is frequently taught that the first one tenth of any money earned should be used for tithing. It is also taught that the second tenth of one's earnings or wages should be saved or invested. This leaves eighty percent (80%) of one's remaining earnings to be used for consumption and lawful pleasure. This is a winning formula.

Business professionals and economists have frequently taught us that if an individual begins saving about fifty dollars per month at the age of twenty-five, he or she would have accumulated moderate savings by their early fifties. The above is attainable because of the act of compounding. Compounding, or interest rate compounding is a mathematical fact that is well proven.

My advice to the young, or individuals entering the workforce are two-fold. First, begin a consistent saving plan early in your life, and second, avoid illegal activities at all costs.

CHAPTER 2

PERSEVERANCE

Except for playing a game of chance such as a lottery, where it is not uncommon for an individual to win playing his or her first game or buying his or her first lottery ticket and realizing a large financial win, success generally comes to people that have the audacity and tenacity to persevere. Perseverance is one of the trademarks of successful people.

Perseverance usually means doing things one has to do, even when they do not feel like doing it. Perseverance can also mean doing unpopular things or jobs when support by one's family and friends is absent, or the event or job is rather unpopular.

In the field of education, perseverance can and does mean staying or remaining at an institution of higher learning when the environment is not what you are accustomed to.

Of course, the power of perseverance only pays dividends when the activities being undertaken are positive ones which can yield positive returns together with the personal and professional fulfillment and achievements.

The power of perseverance would be meaningless, worthless or unproductive if the activity or activities undertaken are unproductive or illegal. For instance, the power of perseverance is meaningless if one's activities pertain to the buying and selling of illegal drugs. Perseverance is without meaning if one's activities involve prostitution related activities.

One might counter with the argument that prostitution is the oldest profession in the world and that it was mentioned in the Holy Bible, but it should never be forgotten that prostitution is seldom a profession that many of its participants are proud of.

In fact, most former prostitutes upon attaining a certain age and level of maturity are usually ashamed of their former occupations.

One's ability to persevere, or the power of perseverance is only productive and rewarding when the activities undertaken are lawful and respectful.

As an attorney, I have represented many individuals charged with a variety of crimes. One of the things that I usually say to them is that they need to change their friends or location and find themselves a different profession, occupation or a different way of earning an income, if possible.

THE BENEFITS OF PERSEVERANCE

The reputation that one has can either be a good reputation, which in many ways would serve to open many doors in many places for him or her; or it can be a bad reputation which would have the opposite effect of a good reputation.

It can rightfully be said that one's reputation precedes them, or that one's reputation follows them. No matter how one looks at it, perseverance if used in a legal or lawful activity or activities bestow upon the participant great rewards.

CHAPTER 3

CONSISTENCY AND PERSEVERANCE IN EDUCATION

It is safe to say or conclude that one cannot become a medical doctor if he or she lacks the ability to persevere. What are the educational requirements for becoming a medical doctor? First one must earn a bachelor's degree, earning respectable grades before he or she can have a realistic expectation of being accepted into a medical school.

Secondly, after obtaining his or her bachelor's degree, most or all medical schools require their applicants to take the Medical College Admission Examination (MCAT). One must also perform reasonably well on that examination if he or she has a reasonable expectation of being admitted to medical school.

After completion of one's bachelor's degree with good grades and an acceptable grade point average and performing well on the MCAT, the third task to be achieved or completed is one's application to medical school.

Unlike law school admission, where personal interviews with the admitting university is not required, one of the protocols of many medical school admission is a personal interview with the medical college.

All the above processes would occur even before the student or applicant is accepted to the medical school. Such a laborious process would serve to weed out the people that are not serious about becoming medical doctors.

WHAT IS PERSEVERANCE?

Perseverance is defined in many dictionaries as "the quality of being persistent". In the case of persisting in positive activities, it can be defined as "continuing in a state of grace leading to a state of glory".

The average man's definition of perseverance would most likely be "to try hard and continuously in spite of obstacles and difficulties." This is a good definition of perseverance, but it should not be forgotten that perseverance in a wrong or illegal activity or activities can be detrimental to one's health and wellbeing and can yield undesirable consequences.

The term perseverance by its very nature does not imply quick or easy success, or quick and easy financial windfalls. However, it is my belief that the rewards realized from years or decades of perseverance in and of itself are much more rewarding than reaping a huge and immediate bounty in a game of chance.

I can recall that after completion of my bachelor's degree and achieving my commission of Second Lieutenant in the U.S. Army Reserve/ Army National Guard, I explained to my Internship Coordinator my plans to attend graduate school, attain my master's degree and upon completion of my master's degree, my intention was to apply to and attend law school. He looked at me and said, "Young man, you have stick-to-ism." To this day, I do not know what he meant when he told me that I have "stick-to-ism." In hindsight, the only reasonable conclusion of his statement is that he was referring to perseverance.

WHAT PERSEVERANCE DOES NOT MEAN?

Being able to persevere does not in any way mean that one would not have struggles. Struggles are a part of living on this earth, and everyone would experience it at least one or more times in their life here on the earth. Even Jesus, during his short life on this earth, underwent many setbacks, heartaches and heartbreaks. In fact, it was Jesus who said, "In this world you will have trouble. But take heart. I have overcome the world." (John 16:33). Jesus reminded us that He had overcome the world, and that with courage, perseverance and persistence we would also do well and achieve our own goals and levels of success in this world.

11

However, we must also remember that this world will not last forever. Nothing in the world is forever, and our successes and failures would also not be forever. This world is not our home, we are only passing through. Our eternal home awaits us after this life is through.

Based on Bible teachings, our eternal home would also bear some traits or representations of how we spend our years in this, our earthly home in our earthly bodies. One thing is certain, with one hundred percent probability, and that is our eternal home is awaiting us, and we will be in that home someday.

CHAPTER 4

TOO SOON OLD & TOO LATE SMART

For the majority of the seven or eight billion people currently residing on the planet earth, the phrase, "too soon old and too late smart" is very applicable to their lives. Many may disagree with me, citing policy issues, class issues, gender issues and racial issues. However, it is my belief that no matter what curve ball life throws our way, there is a way out of it. To me, there is no such thing as "no way out." In most instances the underlying factor depends on how hard and for how long one is willing to work to achieve their goals.

In every society there are people that were dealt a bad hand, and in some cases a terrible hand, that have earned their way out of it. It is also true that economic, political, racial, gender and immigration status do play significant roles in one's access to his or her success, but the bottom line remains how hard one is willing to work to achieve their goals.

I can recall a study that was done by an esteemed university in the United States in the middle of the 1980s. According to the findings of that study, one's race and their education level or background is the primary or key variable that determines success in the United States of America. The findings of this study could be a double-edged sword for the United States of America. For example, what would eventually become of the United States if the educational level of the white population takes a sharp decline? What will the United States of America look like when and if minorities residing in the United States finally realize that their primary track to success is a good education. Would that mean that the United States of America once again becomes engaged in a racial and economic civil war? The variable race has serious long-term implications for stability, sustainability and longevity of the United State Society. Can America maintain its world leadership status if a certain percentage of its population is producing under their full potential due to man-made obstacles?

What would America's economic, military and social position on the world stage be if race is still the primary or main variable in the determination of success? Would America's economic growth and world position be sustainable? Would the US economy be sustainable?

When discussing these topics, one must not forget the intricate role played by the legal system in maintaining or modifying the political and economic system. It is true, that pursuant to the United States Constitution, courts are forbidden from deciding political questions or issues. Political questions are usually held by courts to refer to matters dealing with a particular party's own internal affairs. However, it is my belief that almost any questions or action undertaken by a sufficiently large number of people can be construed as having political implications or influences the economy and the stream of interstate commerce.

POLITICAL QUESTION DOCTRINE

According to the Legal Information Institute (LII), "Federal Courts will refuse to hear a case if they found that it presents a political question. This doctrine refers to the idea that an issue is so politically charged that federal courts which are typically viewed as the apolitical branch of government, should not hear the issue. This doctrine is also referred to as the Justiciability doctrine, or the non-justiciability doctrine".

APPLYING THE DOCTRINE

In Oetjen v. Central Leather Co. (1918) which is one of the earliest examples of the Supreme Court applying The Political Question Doctrine, the Court found that the conduct of foreign relations is the sole responsibility of the Executive Branch. As such, the Court found that cases which challenge the way in which the Executive uses the power present political questions. Thus, the Court held that it cannot preside over these issues." (Legal Information Institute).

The Court broadened this ruling in Baker v. Carr (1962). When it held that Federal Courts should not hear cases which deal directly with issues that the constitution makes the sole responsibility of the Executive Branch and, or Legislative Branch.

The Court in Nixon v. United States (1993) also extended this doctrine to which lawsuits which challenge the Legislative Branch's procedure for impeachment proceedings.

What would the outcome be if a significantly large number of minorities forego pursuing higher education, progression and other ways of upward mobility in a significantly enough quantity? Would that mean the United States of America would once again become a developing nation?

The above issues may appear as simple and unimportant to the average man, but the end result can be significant or catastrophic. Would America revert to encouraging immigration only from predominantly white nations?

All of the above-mentioned issues are significant and important in today's society, but it is not as significant and important as it could become two or three decades from today. My advice for the younger generation is to pursue your dreams, do what you like doing, educate yourself, and remember that word perseverance, and what it means to persevere. Of course, at all times, remember there is a Maker that has created the universe. He is the owner of this universe and without him life can or would be meaningless. Everything in this Universe is owned by him.

JOHN D. CADORE

CHAPTER 5

HAVING AND KEEPING A POSITIVE ATTITUDE

It is believed by many that a positive and respectful attitude can take one as far or even further than a good education. Author Joyce Meyer once said, "a bad attitude is like a flat tire, if you don't change it, you won't go anywhere".

In Shakespearean language, this pun is very applicable to real life. A pun, as defined by William Shakespeare, is described as a play upon words. The dramatic irony of this statement is that she is using this metaphor of a vehicle with a flat or punctured to analogize one's level of attainment or lack of achievement in life.

Does that mean that one should never be angry or get angry? The answer to this question is resoundingly no. As we may recall, Jesus Christ was angered at the Synagogue, when he accused the scribes and pharisees of turning the "House of Worship into a Den of Thieves."

In the Book of Matthew, Chapter 21:13 reads as follows:

"Then Jesus went into the temple of God, drove out all those who bought and sold in the Temple, and overturned the table of the money changers and the seats of those who sold doves."

Jesus then went on to say, "It is written that my house shall be called a house of prayer, but you have made it into a den of thieves."

I quoted This passage from the Book of Matthew in the New Testament for two distinct reasons. First, anger, or being angry in and of itself does not constitute a sin. Anger or being angry over a circumstance can be a very positive tool if channeled into the right direction or arena. I have heard it said by many preachers, that anger is the first step to real and positive change.

However, there exists a major difference between someone that gets angry occasionally and someone that is constantly angry. Consistent anger is a sign of a lack of inner peace and severe internal turbulence. Being consistently angry is bad in and of itself. Persistent and consistent anger is an outward manifestation of inner turbulence. This sort of anger can be and usually is dangerous for one's own health.

According to the Holy Bible, Proverbs 14:29, "Whosoever is slow to anger has great understanding, but he who has a hasty temper exalts folly". Proverbs 15:18 also stated, "A hot tempered man stirs up strife, but he who is slow to anger quiets contention."

Having and keeping a positive attitude does not in any way mean that there will never be periods of anger. However, anger should be controlled to the fullest extent humanly possible. Even Jesus, the only man in the history of mankind that was sinless and blameless, experienced occasional anger when he witnessed and observed misuse of his Father's House of Worship, and when there was misuse and abuse of individuals by other individuals.

According to the Bible, not all anger is wrong. Righteous anger stems from an anger that arises when we witness an offense to God or his Word.

Let us remember James 1: 19-20, "my dear brother and sisters, take note of this: Everyone should be quick to listen, slow to speak and slow to become angry." However not all anger can be classified as being sinful. In short, one can never or rarely be wrong by having and keeping a positive attitude.

CHAPTER 6

ADVERSITY

It is my belief that adversity represents the back door to success. According to author Napoleon Hill, "every adversity ... carries with it the seed to an equal or greater benefit." Based on my life experiences, I would agree with that statement. It is my experience that every adversity carries with it the opportunity to greatly overcome whatever adversity an individual may encounter.

However, it has also been my experience that in order to capitalize on any major adversity, one must first be in the proper state of mind. It is also my belief and my experience that wealth, riches or poverty are all the result of one's state of mind. Starting from the premise that one will be tomorrow what he or she thinks today, or in layman's language, one will become what they are studying or thinking today, it can be easily seen or visualized why wealth, riches or poverty almost always begins with a state of mind.

Now, I do understand that many people realize immediate wealth by engaging in activities such as playing the lottery. However, as statistics will readily reveal, seven out of every ten individuals that achieve such overnight wealth by either playing the various types of lotteries, or gambling at the casino will go broke or lose their wealth within years.

This fact leads us right back to the Bible. Proverbs 21:20, "A fool and his money are soon parted." It is also very important to recognize money or wealth cannot buy happiness, and are unable to grant us peace of mind. The important non-monetary qualities that can and do contribute to health, wealth and peace of mind, in my belief, are positive relationships, primarily with Almighty God, a good and loving family which in most cases can be translated to mean a godly family, a marketable education and reliable friends. A marketable education does not only mean a formal college or university education. A marketable education can be found in a trade or in any other craft which allows an individual to earn a lawful and honest living.

THE BLESSINGS OF DISAPPOINTMENTS

An old friend recently sent me a good night message., "Life is very interesting. In the end some of your greatest pains can become some of your greatest strengths." This is one of the mysteries of life and according to King Solomon, "the wisest man who ever lived," this is "life under the sun."

One must always remember that disappointments are a way of life and that failure in most instances is the back door to success. It is also my belief that the average individual usually learns more from failure than from success. For this reason, it is beneficial for most people to first experience failure in one or two significant events before realizing long term stable success.

There are also many sayings within the Christian community that address the situation. One such saying is, "The bigger the challenge, the greater will be the prize." Another related Biblical saying is, "Through the fire through the flood, before one may arrive at their happy and wealthy place."

All of these sayings are alluding to the fact that happiness and success are not usually quickly and/or readily attained. That in life as we know it, we can expect some, or many, disappointments. However, the key to becoming successful is to stay the course. Staying on the course means that one must be consistent and be willing and ready to persevere.

CHAPTER 7

PERSEVERANCE IN THE FACE OF DISCOURAGEMENT

There is an old saying, "Where determination exists, an individual will always find his or her way." This has proven to be true in almost all situations and in almost all walks of life, and among all nationalities and among all races.

This saying is what I refer to as "mind power" and "will power." Mind power encompasses one's ability to pull their way through very difficult situations without ever seriously considering surrender, quitting or giving up. There is another old saying that "a winner never quits and a quitter never wins".

Life experiences have frequently taught me that success usually builds upon itself. Realizing modest success, in my estimation, is the tool that is needed to overcome lack of self-confidence or little self - confidence. The attainment of moderate and gradual success in various endeavors in my belief, is one of the key ingredients to overcoming low self- confidence.

Another key element needed to persevere in

the face of significant discouragements is "mind power." Mind power is very similar to will power in that one usually cannot exist without the other. Mind power is the characteristic that allows someone to envision themselves crossing the finish line in whatever they endeavor, while others may barely envision themselves starting the same or similar mission.

It should be remembered that the road to success is always under construction. Hence, only the very determined will finish the journey. That is perhaps the reason I am frequently turned off by the word "easy." The word "easy" frequently conveys the implication that the result would not be rewarding or fulfilling. Could it be because as I was taught by my father that nothing good or worthwhile would come easy?

Whenever I hear the word "easy," there is an implicit turnoff that occurs deep within me. Is it because I am a black male immigrant in the United States, and life's lessons have taught me that if anything is easy, then everyone can have it? Or is it that life experiences have taught me that if something is easy and rewarding then there is a high probability that the opportunity would be given to someone else? Or is it a combination of both? For whatever reason or reasons, it may be, the word easy is usually one of my biggest and quickest turn offs.

One's confidence is built by a series of modest successes, with each success in a different undertaking serving to add, foster or enhance one's level of confidence. It would not be uncommon for reasonable people to ask why mind power or willpower is an important characteristic for perseverance.

Mindpower and willpower are both very important because they both will determine the level of difficulties one will or can endure to accomplish his or her goals.

Mindpower and willpower are also significant factors in determining one's level of confidence. One's self-confidence and one's self-esteem are very closely linked. In the field of economics, they would be viewed as being complementary, or as complementary goods. When faced with tremendous obstacles, it should never be forgotten that it is darkest just before dawn. Something that is usually forgotten during periods of hard and dark times is the tougher the obstacles, the more rewarding would be the victory. Favoritism, although desired by many, does not foster strength and great inner or inward satisfaction. There is an inner quality in mankind that can only be achieved through hard work and perseverance. This cannot be handed to anyone.

CHAPTER 8

APPRECIATION

The word appreciation simply means to raise the value of something or someone. The word depreciation has the reverse effect. In short, depreciation means the reduction in value. This term is commonly associated with vehicles. It is common knowledge that whenever one purchases a new vehicle, it depreciates at least ten percent once it is driven out of the dealer's parking lot. Conversely most houses appreciate over time. That is why it is believed that real estate is a long-term investment. The longer one maintains ownership of their real property the greater the probability that income or profits would be realized. That is of course unless there is not a burst or depression in the general real estate market.

Showing appreciation to others is one of the signs of a contented and happy person. There is no need to engage in the practice of tearing others down, because by doing so one is directly or indirectly tearing themselves down. There is an old saying, whenever you help someone rise higher, you rise with them. Conversely whenever one engages in the practice of tearing others down, most times, unknowingly, they are also directly or indirectly tearing him or herself down.

Life is not a zero-sum game. The notion that one must lose in order for someone else to win is simply dysfunctional thinking. Many of the wealthiest people in the world have become financially wealthy by improving the lives of the masses. If you serve the masses, you will live with the classes. If you serve the classes, you will live with the masses.

One such person was Henry Ford. Henry Ford became a wealthy man and a household name by the perfection of mass production of the automobile. By doing so, he improved the lives of many and in the process improved his own life.

Appreciation does not only take the form of financial rewards. Saying thank you to the clerk at the grocery store or the gas station can help to improve their work experience on that day. Even in today's world of sexual harassment, it is not uncommon to improve someone's day by letting the know what a pleasant disposition they carry and your appreciation of their outstanding attitude and/or service.

It is my belief that society in general would be greatly improved and enhanced in a positive way when it becomes part of our routine habits to compliment each other. I am referring to honest compliments and not flattery in order to achieve some material or non-material gain.

However, it is a well-known fact that offering compliments to others is not in everyone's DNA. For whatever unknown reason, it is very difficult for some people to offer compliments to others. It is also very difficult for some people to say, "I love you." That is not because of malice or ill will or jealous feelings. This is just who they are. However, it is my belief that if seventy percent of the people in the world would regularly compliment each other, the world as we know it would become a radically different place.

Being able to compliment one another is not a sign of weakness. It is a sign of strength and self-assurance. Remember that life is not a zero-sum game. Someone does not have to lose for another to win. We can all win together.

CHAPTER 9

GREATNESS

It may not be believed by many, but it is much harder to fail than it is to succeed. Failure in almost all instances is the back door to success. Failure serves to open up new avenues that one never foresaw or never thought existed. One can truthfully say that it is possible to fail oneself to success.

Failure is a catalyst that many people would have never known existed had it not been for disappointments. It is difficult for anyone to say that they have really lived without experiencing failure. What is meant by saying that failure is more difficult to achieve than success, is unless one quits or gives up during their experience of failure, they would recover.

Failure allows people the opportunity to see all or mostly all of the avenues before or in front of them that will lead to success. It's my belief that everyone should experience some degree of failure at least twice in their lifetime.

Prolonged success, although desired by many, can and may usually result in people becoming lackadaisical and, in some instances, taking their eyes off the ball. In that sense failure is usually helpful to redirect individuals to the straight and narrow path, whatever that may be.

For some people, the straight and narrow path may be returning to Christianity. For others it may be becoming a more astute businessman or businesswoman. Still for others, it may be reunification with their family or friends. Whatever one's straight and narrow may be, failure can be a tool to redirect and remobilize one to achieve their ultimate goal, whatever that goal may be.

Although it may sound unrealistic to many, people should also feel grateful for experiencing failure in their lives. The Golden Rule of Failure is to never quit. There is an age-old saying that "quitters never win and winners never quit." The validity of this statement would be left to the reader's life experiences.

Many athletes, including myself, had unpleasant experiences in their first big race, or in their first major soccer match. What will you do? Would you quit sports because of a humiliating loss, or would you train harder and smarter while refining your competitive techniques?

It is my belief that no one truly knows who the fastest man in the world is, or the strongest man in the world. The fastest man in the world or the strongest man in the world is usually not in the competition that is handing out the titles, trophies and medals. The fastest or strongest man in the world may be sitting next to you in history or math class in college or university. They may be on the job working in a factory or they may be an engineer or construction worker.

However realistic or unrealistic that title may be, it is a nice title to have and would usually create a major boost to the title's holder's ego and confidence. Once again, the true test of that title is how it is utilized for the betterment and benefit of many people. There is an old saying in sports, that "the champion makes the title," meaning that the relevancy and prestige of any title would depend on the quality of the person holding that title. The champion makes the title. The title usually does not make the champion.

There is another old saying, that it is more noble to fail than it is to succeed. There is yet another old saying that one learns more from losing than from winning. Although there are truths to all those sayings, most people, or people in general, would prefer to win, rather than to lose. Some people may even go as far as giving their right arm to experience the thrill of winning. Winning brings along a glorious and splendid experience, but it is my belief that the experience of winning, in whatever arena, may be the most enhanced and would be more cherished if one had first experienced the agony of defeat before raising the winner's trophy.

CHAPTER 10

COMMITMENT

The word commitment, which is defined in the Webster's New Collegiate Dictionary as "the act or process of pledging or binding to a certain course or policy," plays a crucial role in perseverance.

For anyone to be willing or able to persevere, they must first be committed to the endeavor to be undertaken. Hence one's commitment should always be to something of value. Something that can add value to oneself or to the lives of others. Value does not have to be monetary; it can be improvement to a social or economic good, such as education, health or wisdom.

The Biblical definition of wisdom is the "favor of the Lord." Fearing the Lord may or may not confer immediate tangible benefits, but from a Christian or faith-based perspective, it would guarantee or generate its rewards in the life to come. It is believed by many that fear of the Lord is the beginning of wisdom.

Once a commitment is made, the person who made the commitment should see it through. However, there are times and occasions when it would not be advisable to fulfill one's commitment, and it would be within the interest of justice to renege on that commitment.

One such example may be when a commitment is obtained by fraud or duress. It is almost never profitable or worthwhile to fulfill any commitment that is obtained by fraud or duress. This concept can be seen in matrimonial law, where annulments are allowed for marriages that were entered into utilizing fraud and duress.

Within matrimonial law, an annulment of a marriage can be construed to mean that the act of matrimony never came to fruition or never existed. Therefore, there was never a marriage; or a valid legal marriage never existed.

The same concept is present in contract law. In order for a valid contract to exist, there must be an offer, acceptance and valid consideration or value exchanged by the parties. Within contract law, the notion of consideration is usually in monetary terms, meaning in dollars and cents.

A MEETING OF THE MINDS

For a commitment to be binding and worthwhile, it must be honestly entered into. Truth and honesty are the most invaluable qualities that must be present whenever a commitment is made or entered into.

Within the context of contract law, it is referred to as a meeting of the minds. Hence, if any party during contract negotiations was less than truthful about the consideration to be received or the subject matter of the underlying contract, or at least one of the parties signed a written contract based upon a misrepresentation of a material element of the contract, then the contract may either be void, meaning that no contract ever existed. Or it can be voidable, meaning the contract can be set aside or rendered invalid by a court of law.

As stated earlier, the three elements required for a legally enforceable contract between the parties to exist are an offer, an acceptance and consideration. In many jurisdictions, consideration can only be in legal tender, meaning currency or currency substitute. A currency substitute can be construed to mean anything that is liquid and can readily or easily be converted into cash or a legal tender. Hence, in many jurisdictions, personal services to be rendered by one party to the contract is unacceptable.

A commitment, for it to be binding, must be for something meaningful and worthwhile to the person making the commitment. Also, of tremendous importance is keeping one's commitment once they are properly made.

CHAPTER 11

DECISIVENESS

Decisiveness is described in Webster's dictionary as "having the power to decide, or "marked by firm determination", or "beyond doubt" is another key element necessary for one to be consistent, and eventually to be persuasive. There is an old saying in the United States Army that making "no decision is worse than making a wrong decision." The notion that underlies that train of thought is that a wrong or bad decision can almost always be corrected, but by not making a decision, there is no beginning point to effectuate necessary changes.

President Ronald Reagan somewhat debunked the above by saying, "making a bad deal is much worse than making no deal." It is my recollection that President Ronald Reagan made that statement when he was contemplating a nuclear arms control treaty with the former Soviet Union.

Within the realm of full disclosure, I must disclose that I received my commission as a military officer under the presidency of Ronald Reagan. Additionally, under the presidency of Ronald Reagan, I achieved the most material success during my residency within the United State of America.

Many people have called the intellect of President Ronald Reagan into question, but the one trait of President Reagan that may not be called into question was his decisiveness in decision making. Decisiveness in decision making is one of the characteristics of good leadership and one of the characteristics required for success in about every arena of life and in almost every profession.

However, there are some elements that are required before making a decision. The first element is information. The question here is, does the decision maker have enough credible information to render a decision? Decisions should never be made for the sole reason of making a decision. A decision, for it to be good, must improve the life of the majority of people whom it will affect. It is almost never a good idea to make a decision solely for the sake of doing so.

Prior to decision making, the sources of information must be properly scrutinized. The bottom line of any decision is that it should improve the lives, comfort level and welfare of the majority of people that will be affected by it.

The art of being decisive is a requirement in order for one to be consistent and in order for one to persevere.

CHAPTER 12

CONTRADICTION AND PROCRASTINATION

Contradiction is described in Webster's dictionary as "a contrary assertion, or inconsistency with itself". It is written in the Bible that a household that is divided amongst itself cannot stand. Mark 3:25, states, if a house is divided against itself, it cannot stand. Jesus himself said that "a house divided cannot stand."

For one to persevere in any activity or endeavor in life, there must be consistency and to a very large degree, the lack of doubt. The presence of doubt usually results in people's second guessing themselves, which in many instances results in procrastination.

The word procrastination is described as in Webster's dictionary as "to put off doing something to a later date." Contradiction usually leads to procrastination which in turn frequently results in diminished or reduced prosperity, wealth or earnings.

Contradiction and procrastination are not positive traits. In fact, some people may say that they are both works of the devil. According to some Bible scholars, procrastination can affect all at times, but it is important to remember that it can cause much damage later. Putting things off for later when they should or can be done now can impact people other than yourself.

There are many reasons people procrastinate. Some of the most common reasons cited or given for procrastination are fear, anxiety, or an unwillingness to face change. It is also believed by many that "the fear of success" can be one reason why people procrastinate.

According to Proverbs 10:4, "A slack hand causes poverty, but a hand of diligence makes you rich." In layman's language, the Bible is saying that procrastination can lead and does lead to poverty.

In short, consistency, perseverance and appreciation are inconsistent with the notion of contradiction and procrastination. Hence success in any field or endeavor requires consistency and the absence of procrastination.

CHAPTER 13

COMPLAINTS AND ARGUMENTS

Frequent complaining and arguing very often will serve to destroy and undermine the citizenry's trust and confidence in the civic system, governmental system, and even the religious system. Frequent complaints represent rebellion against the system of government, civic system or any other system which is the target of the complaints.

Please note that I am not talking about meritorious complaints of injustice, prejudice, bigotry or any of the other malice that regularly rear their ugly heads in our daily lives. Meritorious complaints and criticism serve to create a better and more fair and just society, whereas non-meritorious complaints may serve to weaken the faith and confidence of citizens in the governments or civic organizations.

Of tremendous importance is the idea that complaints and critics of the organization, government or system, should not only have complaints or criticism, but that they should also present solutions and ways to improve whatever they perceive to be broken, or unfair, or unjust about the situation, organizations or government.

The second part of that arm is that those in authority should be willing and ready to act on the complaints of the citizenry. Such actions may include making changes, even systemic changes when warranted. The goal or purpose of any government should be to maximize the welfare of the majority of its citizens. This concept is also true for any organization, whether public or private. Maximizing benefits to its members would serve to not only quiet complaints, but it will also serve to increase the sustainability of the organizations.

A government or organization that is beneficial to the majority of its members is most likely able to survive sudden unanticipated and unseen shock in the system. Where an organization or government that is unresponsive to the people it serves will most likely be replaced whenever an opportunity presents itself. This is exactly what occurred in the disappearance of the United Soviet Socialist Republics as a political entity and a government.

The former Soviet Union was primarily only responsive to white males, despite many other races and ethnic groups within its borders. Hence, due to its lack of responsiveness and exclusion of many of its citizens, the government was unable to stand the test of time.

For an organization to survive, it must be inclusive of its citizenry, and it must be responsive to the needs of its citizenry. To the best of my knowledge, the Soviet Union, or USSR, was lacking in both areas. The result is that it is no longer present today. Not only that it is no longer in existence, but most of the people that were once part of that system presently find it to be undesirable.

The lesson to be learned here is that both leadership or membership or citizenry play or fulfill unique roles. Such roles are interdependent or codependent. Hence, for such a government or organization to survive, benefits must be realized for each other. It cannot be a one-way stream.

Today we are also witnessing many commonwealth nations discussing whether the role of the British Monarchy is worthwhile. The island nation of Barbados has left the British Commonwealth of Nations. The island of Jamaica is now considering taking similar action as was taken by the island of Barbados. The underlying questions to be asked here are: Was the British Monarchy responsive to the Commonwealth of Nations? Is the British Commonwealth of Nations facing the same fate as the former Soviet Union, or USSR? This question will be answered with the passage of time.

My position is that it is not wrong in and of itself to complain or critique, but it is much more valuable to everyone involved, when or if the complaining parties or individuals can provide solutions to correct the problems.

CHAPTER 14

HABIT

A habit is defined in Webster's dictionary as a "continual, often involuntary or unconscious, inclination to perform an activity, acquired through frequent repetition". A habit can also be described as an established disposition of the mind or character, or customary practice or manner.

In short, all the above definitions of habit are saying the identical thing. In short, a habit is something one is predisposed to perform or do when no one is watching. A good habit is generally done or performed to achieve optimal performance, or to get ahead of the line. It is something or actions undertaken by someone that is predisposed to do so. A habit can also be developed at various stages of life.

The habits of consistency, perseverance and appreciation are all positive traits that when undertaken by anyone would naturally lead to positive self-fulfilling results and outcomes.

For a college or high school student, the habit of studying one or two hours a day would probably and customarily cause you to be on the Dean's list of students with outstanding grade point averages every semester. For an athlete, the habit of training every other day and not using alcohol or tobacco products, or illegal drugs would in all probability extend your athletic life and very probably assist you in becoming one of the most successful athletes in your sport. The use of illegal drugs would not only serve to eliminate you from your chosen sport, but it will also shorten your athletic career. Thus, a good habit for almost all athletes to develop at the very onset of their athletic careers is to say no to all illicit or illegal drugs. Winning is best appreciated when the rules are followed. The idea of cheating in order to win yields no lasting, or even short time glory.

I mentioned training every other day as opposed to training every day because during my time in athletics, it was not encouraged to train every day. Training every other day was the norm. For medical, health and muscular reasons which I do not wish to get into in this book, athletes during my time were encouraged to train every other day.

The bottom line here is that good habits when utilized will yield positive results. On the contrary, bad habits would most likely lead to poor or bad results.

CHAPTER 15

THE COMPANY ONE KEEPS

There is an old saying, "Show me your company, and I will tell you who you are." It is my belief and experience that there is a lot of truth to this statement. The company one keeps should be dependable and law abiding. Being dependable does not in any way mean that they would be agreeable to all of your ideas. It simply means that they would tell you the truth and the facts whether you are agreeable with them or not. It means they are strong enough to tell the facts or situations as they really are, and not just the things that would like to hear. That implies a certain level of stability.

It is not very helpful or advantageous to surround oneself with people less progressive than you are, or by individuals that are able to find employment but refuse to do so. People that are dependent upon you to earn a living should be your employees, not your associates. Being dependent upon anyone to earn a living would or could result in situations where the truth of a situation or adventure may not be revealed for fear of losing financial support.

It is also important that one's associates also have different skill sets. Notably individuals of different professions and of different walks of life. Individuals that have different perspectives on life and can observe a situation from different angles. It is not advantageous to usually be the most knowledgeable person within your circle. Being the most knowledgeable individual within your circle or network would most likely serve to limit your growth. There should be free flowing ideas, mainly different ideas, which are most frequently obtained from being in the midst of people from different professions and from different walks of life. Ideas in many instances can be more valuable than money.

Also, of tremendous importance is avoiding the company of people who speak negatively about you when you are not around. This can be the result of jealousy and envy, which as you know are two of man's original sins. The Bible has taught us that the first case of murder in the world occurred when Cain killed his brother Abel out of jealousy. God accepted gifts and offerings of Abel and rejected the offering of Cain. That incident led to the world's first case of murder.

Another type of person or individuals that should be avoided are people that are more than willing to tear down your character, reputation or your well- being. People of racist dispositions should also be avoided at all costs. This world is a multi-cultural place. Thus, every race and culture should be seen as equally important.

Friends or members of one's inner circle should serve to build him or her up and not to tear them down. That is the notion of the old saying, "speaking truth to power." Speaking truth to power can only occur when one is secure and confident in the wellbeing and in themselves.

In short, one's friend or inner circle should serve to build him or her up, not tear them down. Acquaintances are many, but friends are few. One's friends or acquaintances would usually reveal themselves during periods of adversity. Hence, the adversities we face in life have the general tendencies to make us stronger. This is one of the many reasons why adversities usually have positive long-term effects. Adversities, although almost wholly undesirable, should not be run away from. Things usually would work out well in the end. There is a bright lining behind every dark cloud.

CHAPTER 16

IMPORTANT KNOWLEDGE

There is usually a role to be played by everyone that comes into one's life. Some people's objective is usually to test or challenge us. Others' objective is maybe to use us to obtain something that is valuable to them. However, it should not be forgotten that the role of a certain percentage of the people that come into one's life is primarily to love and support them.

Thus, some people are there to test or challenge you, some people are there to use you to obtain things that they deem is important to them, and others are there to love and support you. The motives of these three categories of people are usually revealed in due course.

It is my hope that the habits laid out in this book will serve to encourage readers to foster good personal relationships. It should always be remembered that for one to see the rainbow, one must first go through the storm.